EDUARDO CARRILLO

EDUARDO CARRILLO

Exhibition Venues:

The Museum of Art & History @ the McPherson Center
August 22 - November 22, 2009
705 Front Street
Santa Cruz, CA 95060
www.SantaCruzMAH.org

Weigand Gallery
January 22 - February 27, 2010
Notre Dame de Namur University
1500 Ralston Avenue
Belmont, CA 94002
www.WeigandGallery.org

Santa Rosa Junior College Art Gallery
September 9 - October 23, 2010
1501 Mendocino Ave., Frank P. Doyle Library
Santa Rosa, CA 95401
www.SantaRosa.edu/art-gallery

Published by *Museo Eduardo Carrillo*
Copyright 2009

ISBN 978-1-61584-315-2

For information please direct inquiries to:
Museo Eduardo Carrillo
Betsy Andersen, Director
PO Box 8085, Santa Cruz, CA 95061
www.MuseoEduardoCarrillo.org

Photography by rr jones: cover jacket, pages 7, 15, 19, 26, 36, 40, 41.
Catalogue design by Marc D'Estout, Santa Cruz, CA

Printed in China

ACKNOWLEDGEMENTS

People's actions often draw our attention. Eduardo was one such person, so filled with attentiveness and flights of fancy.

His art and company compelled not only me, as his student and later his friend, but all those with whom he came into contact.

We wanted these exhibitions to convey his majestic vision and the fullness of his companionship. I feel so gratified by its realization.

And so again, I am reminded of how the actions of individuals have so much to do with this coming about.

Alison Carrillo's vision and that of our Board, especially John Fitz Gibbon, gave structure to Museo Eduardo Carrillo and defined its goal of bringing Eduardo's art and generous legacy into the world. Without reservation, I have only heard affirmation from people when they hear about these plans. Artists, writers, curators, friends and family stand together in the belief that it is a right and fitting endeavor.

We have to thank Paul Figueroa, Executive Director of The Museum of Art & History @ the McPherson Center, for initiating this exhibition and Susan Hillhouse, Curator of Exhibitions and Collections, for giving it life. Thanks to the whole staff at MAH, especially Paula Kenyon, for their seamless work on this project.

A meeting at Alison's with Robert Poplack, Stephanie Sanchez and Deborah Kirklin initiated exhibition plans at their college galleries, and so we are delighted to share Eduardo's art with the visitors to the Weigand Gallery, College of Notre Dame de Namur, Belmont, California and the Santa Rosa Junior College Art Gallery at Santa Rosa, California.

We wish to thank the Boards of the Museum of Art & History @ the McPherson Center, the Weigand Gallery and Santa Rosa Junior College Art Gallery, for their behind the scene commitment, service and vision which shapes our public faces. In particular, we pause to remember Zeb Stewart (1942-2009), painter and advocate for the arts, whose extensive Board service to the Weigand Gallery (1990-2009) ended all too soon.

Thank you to the donors of art and resources for their tangible support. To our designer Marc D'Estout and photographer rr jones who were delightful to work with and always provided a hearty laugh.

To the writers and poets, whose creativity gave us a lens through which to enjoy the work with our other senses. They offer a pathway for our contemplation.

To Alison, whose ease and insight always is expansive.

And to my family, John and Kyra, and Wendy and Donald.

Betsy Andersen
Director
Museo Eduardo Carrillo
Santa Cruz, California

Portrait of Eduardo
Photograph by Edmund Teske, 1960s

"They were surprising in completeness of realization and absolutely convincing in authenticity. In all there was evident his serious inquiry, his bold adventure, his passionate engagement."

As quoted from William Brice, 1997.

AN INTRODUCTION TO EDUARDO CARRILLO

"Oh my gosh!" I exclaimed, as I walked into the studio of Eduardo Carrillo. It was evening, dark and new, and I was alone with the brilliant color, strange and strong images, of large scale paintings by an incredible artist. Hidden in the in foothills of the coastal range of Santa Cruz, the Carrillo residence of Alison and Eduardo is a magical place. Discovery, celebration and astonishment continued to surface during my visits. Initially to meet his widow Alison and then an invitation to join others—curators, artists, patrons and friends, and the Carrillo family—in a birthday celebration of Eduardo's life, it was for me an introduction to the vision for Museo Eduardo Carrillo. Recently arrived from Charleston, South Carolina, and a museum career at one of the South's oldest and most distinguished art museums, I was keenly aware of the importance of place in an artist's works and a museum's role to clearly define and shape a collection reflecting its constituencies.

Since these initial visits, I have learned more and more about Eduardo Carrillo's life and career. At the Museo it was my good fortune to meet John Fitz Gibbon, art historian, professor and collector. That evening he presented an illustrated lecture highlighting California art and Eduardo's place and contributions at the end of the 20th century. There is, to me, a superb example from his talk—*Down the Lane*—a museum quality work resonating with the lifestyle and spirit of California. The composition is filled with action and figures skillfully executed by the artist directly from his experiences in this special place, California. In fact this piece refers to a mecca for the surf culture in Santa Cruz, Steamer's Lane. Additional knowledge surfaced through his contributions to Santa Cruz during his tenure at the University of California, Santa Cruz. With Alison and Betsy Andersen, I was introduced to a large scale, spiritual mural filled with passion and executed with an amazing technique. The outstretched arms and enormous torso once filled the entire passageway of a breezeway in a building along the Pacific Garden mall in downtown Santa Cruz. Many have shared their experience of the mural with me. From photographs and standing in the space, my mind recreated the emotional impact upon viewers produced by the imagination and skills of Eduardo.

Finally, a visit to the National Steinbeck Center in Salinas presented a glimpse into the artist's heritage, his ancestral land of San Ignacio in the Baja region of Mexico. Here was a unique geographic area visited by John Steinbeck and many other 20th century residents of California. Here were Eduardo's family and culture depicted in numerous intimate studies and spontaneous watercolors. Several paintings depicted his friends and relatives. The locale is brought to life through paintings like *Tio Beto on The Wall*. Not only was this a private glimpse into the background of this painter but an awakening to Eduardo's role as a teacher, providing services

Down the Lane
1991-1992
Oil on canvas
71 x 51"
Collection John and Jane Fitz Gibbon

and encouragement for careers and success in his mother's land. A devotion and leadership exemplified his passion and career in Santa Cruz.

On behalf of the Board of Trustees and staff at the Museum it is our pleasure to showcase this Santa Cruz treasure and significant California artist by organizing *Eduardo Carrillo: Within A Cultural Context*. The accompanying educational programs and publication will share with a wider audience the life and impact of Eduardo Carrillo, an internationally renowned painter and muralist. We are most grateful for the interest and generosity of many collectors who have shared Eduardo's work and to the many donors who

generously provided resources to accomplish our goal through the efforts of Susan Hillhouse, Curator of Exhibitions and Collections at the Museum and Betsy Andersen at Museo Eduardo Carrillo. And thank you Alison, so very much, for sharing the legacy of an amazing artist and vibrant person, Eduardo Carrillo.

Paul Figueroa
Executive Director
The Museum of Art & History
@ the McPherson Center,
Santa Cruz, California

4

AFFINITY AND REFLECTION

I was a student at the University of California Santa Cruz when Eduardo Carrillo taught there. By all accounts he was a fantastic teacher. Although I missed the opportunity to study with him, I became familiar with his work after I graduated. I well recall wonderful exhibitions of his paintings at the Joseph Chowning Gallery in San Francisco. I had an affinity with his paintings, especially the small watercolors of everyday life that he painted at his home in Baja. I had spent a year working with a local artisan in Chiapas before I studied at the University of California, Santa Cruz, and I admired how Eduardo's watercolors captured the life of the people in the same way his large mural sized paintings dealt with the cultural aspects of being Hispanic.

Not long after I received my M.F.A., I was at a conference with Deborah Kirklin, a co-curator for this exhibition. We were both looking for teaching jobs and paying our dues. I happened to run into Eduardo and introduced Deborah to him. He looked at her slides, and a few weeks later he called her to see if she would like to teach in the Art Department in the spring quarter. Eduardo seemed to be a good enough judge of character to know what an excellent teacher Deborah would make, and he had the generosity of spirit to give someone untried a chance.

The online Museo Eduardo Carrillo is a testament to the people who cared about Eduardo and his art. It is as much an idea as it is a place. It is significant as a repository for Eduardo's

oeuvre and is proof of its lasting power. Many of the paintings are installed in the home of his wife, Alison Carrillo; his work hangs on every wall. Here you get a sense of the breadth and scope of Eduardo's ever-curious mind. The place is imbued with his spirit. In many ways the Museo extends the ideas about art that were important to Eduardo. With great pride we present Eduardo Carrillo's work at the Wiegand Gallery in conjunction with Santa Rosa Junior College and The Museum of Art & History @ the McPherson Center in Santa Cruz.

Robert M. Poplack
Director, *Wiegand Gallery*
Notre Dame de Namur University
Belmont, California

A PERSONAL VIEW

Ed had a legendary status amongst his cronies, who were my friends, too, in LA in the 90s. Some were well known artists, as was Ed, and had studied with Diebenkorn at the University of California, Los Angeles in the 50s or 60s. Over lunch at Louis Lunetta's (Italian American painter and wild man and son of a baseball star) they reminisced about painting trips to Baja, forays into psychedelia, mural painting at the farmer's market and how Ed was happily married and settled in Santa Cruz teaching. They were grumpy about not seeing him enough.

I needed a job, one of the LA guys called Ed, and I was hired to fill in for him for a semester at the University of California, Santa Cruz. Ed later told me I was hired because of my elipses! Ed was perusing an enormous Rembrandt book, especially the portraits. I wondered how that affected the way he painted campesinos and other friends when he went down to Baja.

Ed and Alison invited me to stay with them in Santa Cruz the two days a week I taught. I found myself using Ed's studio, painting with him on several occasions, sharing still life objects, his a reclining laughing Buddha and an earth red Mexican goblet, mine a stuffed sparrow.

Ed gave me a water color lesson or two, occasionally he sang and played a guitar, spontaneously, naturally.

He'd hand me a pile of his watercolors and say, "Leaf through these, and put them in the order you think is correct from good to bad." He asked me to do this several times that semester, sometimes giving me the same pile of watercolors to 'evaluate.'

Many portraits of Alison were amongst the watercolors, and paintings of her hung in the house. The closeness and intimacy they shared was, like everything else in Ed's life, the subject of his art.

Many a time I saw my hosts holding hands and walking together, deep in conversation. One could literally sit in the kitchen with them in the morning as I did many times and bask in the warmth of their love for one another. It is in the art to see as well.

Stephanie Sanchez
Gallery Director
Santa Rosa Junior College Art Gallery
Santa Rosa, California

Eduardo Carrillo's studio

LUX PERPETUA

Eduardo Carrillo—painter, father, husband, professor—died on July 14, 1997, leaving a rich legacy and a collective broken heart. Born on April 8, 1937, in Los Angeles, Carrillo attended Los Angeles City College before taking his BA and MA degrees at the University of California, Los Angeles. After a year in Spain—studying and painting in the Prado—he and his young family moved to Ed's ancestral home in La Paz, Baja California, where he founded and directed El Centro de Arte Regional. The gifted painter and muralist had already enjoyed many solo exhibitions of his bold artworks in both Mexico and Los Angeles before joining the faculty of the Unuversity of California, Santa Cruz in 1972. There, for the last 25 years of his life, he taught drawing, art history, ceramics, mural, fresco, as well as his primary media of oil and watercolor painting.

Memories of Eduardo always begin with his smile and his astonishing azure eyes. The smile—a permanent possibility of who he was in the world—fed from the same spring as his immense talent. Somehow about light and color, always about irrepressible sweetness and humor, that spring seemed unquench-able. Even now that he's gone, it still seems so. Probably because Ed Carrillo, celebrated, loved, catalogued and anthologized, wore his gift so lightly. He never took it so seriously that it couldn't be suspended while he explored some moment of friendship. Part trickster god, part

transcultural poet, Ed was an inspiration to his students and colleagues alike.

Armed with the instinctive immediacy of a perpetual child—fascinated with the colors, shapes, and rhythms of the sensory world—Ed probed and prodded the land, here and in his beloved Baja, where he'd go each year to putter with a favorite uncle, soak up the light of his grandmother's village, work on a never-ending building project and open himself to inspira-tion. About 21 years ago, a whole new window opened on his life with the meeting of Alison Keeler, who became his second wife. There had been a lot of love in Ed's life, and Alison was its ultimate expression.

Colors for Carrillo existed in the service of light, transforming themselves magically before your very eyes—into the light of an early afternoon in Baja. Here the light is so intense that colors seem twice-distilled, like good tequila, into something potent enough to rediscover what passes for reality. Magic realism. Before the term found currency in literature and film-making, Carrillo was robustly inventing it. Driving the everyday, the humble into mythic moments, painting the human into countless gods—every single one of them capable of simultaneous laughter and destruction.

Ed's figures, always monumental and earthy, were more sculpted than painted. They bore a fundamental sense of physicality that seemed directly descended—or perhaps ascended—

Warrior
1997
Oil on canvas
56 x 46"
Collection Alison Carrillo

from muralists like Rivera and Siqueiros. Solidly grounded in a world that frothed and spiraled around them like dancers in fiesta, or warriors poised to conquer some jungle enemy, his all-too-human subjects seemed to wink even in their martyrdom. Ed's Blessed Virgin sipped coffee with the babes who tempted Quetzalcoatl and seduced Louis Valdez.

The effect of Carrillo's largest masterworks produced the frontera equivalent of Saint Chapelle. But instead of the light being saturated with the hues of stained glass, it is the resonance of enormous canvases—all talking to each other in Carrillo's muscular language of tropical sexuality and archetypal innuendo —that performs the lasting impression. The atmosphere shimmers with burnt oranges, that dried blood mahogany that was his signature, lustrous turquoise and a robust Aztec yellow. Painted in the early to mid-eighties, they are the work of a giant, of the man widely regarded as a leader of American painting, Hispanic and otherwise.

Ed painted and taught like he lived—letting go and surrendering to the fullness of his moment in the universe. Trusting that moment completely. For all of us left in a world without Eduardo Carrillo, his moment was not nearly long enough.

Christina Waters
Professor, Writer and Plein Aire Painter

A CONVERSATION ◆ ◆ ◆

between Alison Carrillo and Susan Hillhouse at the MAH on May 1, 2009.

Please describe the first time you were aware of Eduardo Carrillo. When and where did you meet him?

I first time I laid eyes on Ed Carrillo I was not impressed. He looked unkempt and unwell. The year was 1983, and he was a speaker at a relationship seminar that addressed the differences between men and women. I did not know who he was or anything about him. While he had the audience in stitches, I remember thinking he seemed troubled.

When did your courtship begin?

"This is Ed Carrillo," he said when I answered the telephone. It was 1987. I did not remember him and still did not know who he was, but he was amusing and charming and we talked on the phone every few days for many weeks. I began to look forward to his calls. He told me his name was Eduardo Leonardo Antonio Sanchez Zuniga Carrillo Leree.

You had bright and soulful telephone conversations.

Yes, we told our life stories. He was funny and musical and silly. I laughed my head off! Who was this guy? He wooed me with the Latin Mass. In high school I had studied Latin, and read Virgil and Cicero. I had been raised in a devout Anglican household, and the prayers and plainsong of the old Roman Mass meant something to me. He had been an altar boy at St. Michael's Church in L.A. Epistles and missals, matins and lauds, he knew them all. In his rich warm voice Ed intoned the ancient sounds, and I drew closer. I had spent years practicing yoga and meditation. I was totally keyed into the spiritual and this was seductive. I learned that he loved and respected his mother. That meant everything to me.

In June of 1987, you accepted his invitation for dinner. What did you think this time when you saw him? Were you impressed?

I caught a glimpse of him through the screen, dark, masculine, spent.

NO-O-O-O-O-O-O-O-O-O-O-O-O-O-O-O-O-O! I ignored it. Our lives would never be the same.

After twenty two years of marriage, he and Sheila were split up and he was living in town. I knew nothing about his prowess as a painter; our conversations went elsewhere. But he made me feel comfortable. His humor was subtle and hilarious at the same time. He said things like, "What's good about me is I know what's good." Or, "There isn't anything I can't do, it's just a matter of if I want to." I would soon learn that this was not mere bombast, but the truth. He was a humble fellow with a strong ego, tremendously aware.

Photo by Bhavani Parsons

He was always learning something new. His willingness to not know, to be imperfect, to not have it all together, wielded a powerful influence on me. He was non-judgmental and gave me space to be fully who I am. Naturally, that inspired me to give him the same courtesy.

What were Eduardo's work habits? Did he have a routine in the studio? Did he invite you in to work sometimes?

He was project oriented, and he always had things going on. But he didn't talk about his projects until he was doing them. One day he said, "I'm going to make some stools," and I said, "Oh! Stools, that's a great idea," thinking they would be made someday. You know, he would just make things out of odd materials, totally made up design, so it was interesting, whatever he did, to see how he did it. And then at the end of the day, he walked into the house with a couple of stools, and I said, "Oh, you made stools today?!" He was like that, he didn't tell you if he was thinking about something or, you know, getting excited about something. But then when he was doing it, or had just done it, he would show it to you.

He crafted a series of music boxes for his family, beautiful, strong, wooden boxes, lined them with felt and put in little motors for music. And then he painted them with pastoral scenes in subtle muted tones.

What was it like being married to an artist? The day-to-dayness of it?

When I think about my life with Ed I remember the deep peace and pleasure of our days. He so much loved the things he was doing; he loved the home life. He loved being loved. The mood around the house was mirthful.

It meant a lot to him for us to have time together, and he took as many sabbaticals from the University as he could. Sometimes he was able to string two together, and with summers off, he would have months to paint, to travel to his studio in Baja, to work in his garden, to unwind and enjoy a simple life at home.

He took a lot of pleasure in the things that he did everyday. He was always trying something new and different. He enjoyed being in the unknown and having to solve problems. That's what the canvas represented to him, infinite problems, decisions, resolutions.

Ed always had at least one oil in process in his studio. He would paint to a certain point and then settle into his big comfy chair and just look at it for the longest time, squinting and contemplating the work.

I took food to him in his studio. He was starting to pay attention to his diabetes so we did a lot of good eating. I modeled for him as much as I could. That was really some of our most fun days: modeling and eating and playing music. Ed was a natural musician. Very bold and rhythmic, completely untrained. He played his mandolin every day and sang the old love songs, Los Panchos, from the '40s. If there were any children or dogs around, they were welcome. His studio was a place he spent a lot of time and the door was always open. He often played Gershwin or Beethoven or Coltrane loudly while he painted. He didn't need to have outer silence necessarily; he could create an inner silence. He was able to focus and concentrate.

I loved modeling for Ed. He was a rigorous observer. I liked looking at him looking at me. At first I was a bit intimidated. While he was taking my body apart with his eyes, what was he seeing? He was in his world of light and dark, warm and cool, space and depth—things I knew nothing about. I was in my meditation feeling the intimacy, feeling known. His concentration precluded conversation.

I was challenged to settle into a pose I could keep. An unaligned pose quickly turns to agony. He was always protective of me and would call a break every 15 minutes. The earliest stages of a painting invariably looked horrible to me, very crude, amateurish, embarrassing even. He said, "painting is moulding," as he added another layer. He had confidence in his process and never worried about what it looked like.

He just went into beginner's mind and painted. When it was at a certain point he would bring it into the house, hang it in the living room and sit and look at it for a long time.

Was the time spent working on watercolors his reflective time? Time for getting centered?

Sure, the watercolors were a meditation in the morning. They did center him, and they got him focused where he wanted to be. He would wake up by 5 am, make a cup of coffee and sit down in the kitchen with his watercolors. Before breakfast, he would have completed two or three. I would come downstairs and find him warm, soft and quiet.

So, he was an easy-going person with a sweet personality?

Yes, he wasn't a person who blamed others or had grudges or axes to grind, he didn't carry around stuff that interfered with his upbeat temperament. There were endless spontaneous moments of pure hilarity.

All he ever gave me was positive, kind appreciation. In the ten years I knew him, he never criticized me once. I never heard a single thoughtless remark come out of his mouth about me or anyone, really. He was a great listener and could always offer helpful insights. Our communication was loving and safe. That's how it felt with Ed, very emotionally safe. For me it was heaven.

Did teaching sustain him emotionally and creatively as well as financially?

He enjoyed teaching; he enjoyed the students, and he was a very good teacher. He had a way of making simple and concise observations that were liberating to the students. He could see their strengths and was able to help them build on those strengths. He was positive and kind with them. Students are just out of the cradle, so to speak, and he understood that their egos were fragile, and he wanted to inspire them to paint.

As a serious painter, was he patient and open to having students who were non-art majors in his class?

He didn't think art was just for serious, good painters. He really felt that everyone has creativity and lots to give. I know he respected and genuinely liked students. There was a lot of warmth both ways; he invited them to our home and made sure they always felt welcome and special. It was really lovely.

What did he not enjoy about teaching?

One thing he didn't like about the University was the committees, and all the politicking. That was not his cup of tea; but after twenty-five years he got quite good at it, he got good at carrying the load lightly, so that he didn't let the pressures that built up there weigh him down too much. At the end of the day he could leave them behind.

I know he was disturbed at some of the changes that occurred over the years and angered at persistent efforts to take away funding for drawing and painting. There were other programs coming in at the time. He thought students needed to know how to draw and paint, no matter what area of art they wanted to focus on. And, overwhelmingly, the students wanted the basic courses. But he had to struggle against the forces to keep the meager funding allotted to his field.

He was always eager to come home. He'd come rolling in before 5 o'clock pm, take off his school clothes, put on his painting clothes, kiss me hello, share a little something, then go out to his studio and paint before dinner.

When he was offered early retirement, he did not accept. At that point he entered into a really rewarding phase; the last five years with his students were the best, very special.

What else would you like people to know about Ed?

Eduardo was not only a great painter, but a great man. He loved painting, his family, San Ignacio. He spent no time promoting himself. During his dying days he said that he figured the most important thing is to help people. Well, he helped me and just about everyone else he knew, in one way or another. He was a unique blend of discipline and commitment with an unrelenting humorous view of the world. As Francisco Alarcon said so perfectly, "un verdadero caballero con la locura que cura," a true gentleman with the madness that heals. I miss him.

Susan Hillhouse
Curator of Exhibitions and Collections
The Museum of Art & History
@ the McPherson Center,
Santa Cruz, California

Bhavani Parsons, Sage Hodgetts, Alison Carrillo, Eduardo Carrillo

Living room at Eduardo and Alison Carrillo's home

PAINTING LIFE

El Chinaco
1982
Oil on canvas
67.5 x 60"
Collection Ruben Carrillo

The amount of work and the breadth of images that Eduardo Carrillo created were not apparent to all of us who knew him at the university. He was understated, nurturing, and easy in his demeanor. When looking at his work I "get" the outrageousness of living, while recording your thoughts and impressions in paint and being totally committed to doing it. His paintings have modesty, humor and a biting reserve.

Eduardo's color comes out of his involvement with the paint. It produces a sense of light as well as time and an abundance of pattern. Color plays off color in creating context and image. He paints mythology, history, and everyday life here and in Mexico, transforming it with his personal vision and craft.

In *Las Tropicanas*, a painting with a complex structure, Ed creates an unexpected clash of figures embedded into their environment within his own personal mythology. It's like the Aztecs meeting Las Vegas in LA. Pattern is everywhere. Color is acidic. The toad is central in the image,

fold-out plate

Reaching for Coatlique
1988
Oil on canvas
40.5 x 83"
Collection Juliette Carrillo

holding the space. With one limb raised, it looks unflinchingly at the viewer. There are beautiful women with patterns all over their bodies. One blows smoke out of her mouth in the form of lines conjuring ten skeletons. Another stands facing a hummingbird. An archer lies on the ground, the eyes, two white dots of paint, sear at the viewer.

In the *Flight of Sor Juana,* Sor Juana is flung over the chair; the color—hot pastel. She is in ecstasy beneath the Crucifix. The shadow on the cross above the chest holds the space for Christ's head, but instead we find his face on the chest of the crucified like a tattoo of a modern day Chicano.

A similar humor surfaces in *El Chinaco.* Historically, a Chinaco was a mestizo of humble origins, a guerrelliero who fashioned a place for himself of personal independence and culture. Here in Ed's painting, the figure in its entire splendor rides a strong steed into the sunset.

Reaching for Coatlique. In the myth of the Aztecs, Coatlique is the earth and loving mother producing and consuming everything that

lives. In the painting the two figures are lying, twisting horizontally, she with a snake wrapped around her arm, reaching out. He goes for the snake. His fingers almost touch its head. The patterned cloth sets the space. Simple?

Set around Eduardo's studio sink are tiles rejected from his mural, *El Grito*. Looking at these tiles from his ceramic mural in Los Angeles, one can see the array of strokes that were originally drawn over the surface of the tiles in opaque minerals and earth. There is a wonderful build up of marks, which create the image one square at a time. These marks have the fluidity and transparency of an ink wash drawing.

In *Bali Back from Bali* we see a blonde woman, Alison, his wife, with a sunburned chest,

*Matrimonial Bliss
(The Family)*
1996
Oil on canvas
41.75 x 21"
Collection Alison Carrillo

dressed in the spoils of travel. There are portraits of his kids, Juliette and Ruben, sleeping, reading, and of his friend and colleague, Doyle Foreman. There are many scenes of Mexico, people in the heated shade, the musicians, the brothers fighting, people warming and drumming.

In *Matrimonial Bliss*, a self-portrait, his hands are fluttering above the mandolin. He is strumming and singing with pursed lips. She is dancing. Each is lost in their personal reverie, together.

Roberta Ruiz
Artist and Teacher

A REFLECTION ON SOR JUANA INEZ DE LA CRUZ AND HER PORTRAIT

Sor Juana Inez de la Cruz (1651-1695)

Sor Juana Inez de la Cruz came to new prominence in the late 20th century as the first published feminist of the New World and as the most outstanding writer of the Spanish American colonial period. A woman of genius in the seventeenth century who was renowned for her erudition as a nun, poet and scholar, musicologist and scientist, she is sometimes called the Tenth Muse. For many Chicana and Chicano artists she represented an intellectual and feminist by writing in Spanish, Nahuatl and even in the incantation of the voices of African slaves. Writing of her own self portrait in the Ovillejos she reflects on the artifice of the painter, she chastises the artist for trying to seduce her with false beauty and vanity.

"These lying pigments facing you, with every charm brush can supply, set up false promises of color to lead astray the unwary eye; Here, against ghastly tolls of time, bland flattery has staked a claim, defying the power of passing years to wipe out memory and name. And here, in this hollow artifice, frail blossom hanging on the wind, vain pleading in a foolish cause: poor shield against what fate has wrought, all efforts fail and in the end, a body goes to dust, to shade, to naught, to void.... es cadaver, es polvo, es sombra, es nada."

If she were to see Eduardo Carrillo's painting, *El Vuelo De Sor Juana* with its fluted sleeve, elliptical figure and monastic cell, what would she tell him? Would she see his iconic painting as not an image of her beauty but far more...an image of her historic presence, of her monumental intellect and of her courageous commitment to peoples of the New World? His Sor Juana recalls Bernini's Santa Teresa in an ecstatic state of divine love. This Sor Juana moves us beyond her beauty to the soul of her deepest passion for the written word. This Sor Juana links us to our spiritual tradition of the arts and our place on this continent.

Amalia Mesa-Bains
Artist, Professor and MacArthur Fellow

El Vuelo De Sor Juana
1982
Oil on canvas
96 x 60"
Collection Juliette Carrillo

Guatemote
1983
Oil on canvas
38 x 42"
Collection Ruben Carrillo

The Aerialist
1992
Oil on canvas
76 x 50"
Collection Alison Carrillo

The Young Archeologist
1984
Oil on canvas
24 x 18"
Collection Sheila Carrillo

The Sacred Twins
1984
Oil on canvas
56 x 84"
Collection Donna and Lee Sweatfield

Two Brothers Fighting
1986
Oil on canvas
70 x 88.75"
Collection Ruben Carrillo

A MEDITATION ON TWO BROTHERS FIGHTING

Two Brothers Fighting. It's an old story, yet it continues to this day.

Locked in battle, they tower over the blue and gold-lit landscape, intent on harming each other while defending themselves against pain.

Their bare feet struggle on steps that circle around, ridged and jagged, beginning where they end, and ending where they begin. Perhaps these are remnants of an ancient civilization. Or the conception of a new one.

It's an old story. Even though Cain and Abel are the only two people on earth, they cannot get along.

Am I my brother's keeper?

The two brothers fighting may be Ishmael and Isaac, one bringing death and destruction, the other justice and peace. They may be Jacob and Esau fighting for the spiritual and material legacy of the family. They may be Joseph and his brothers fighting over a dream.

They are larger than life. And yet they are life. They are locked in a life and death struggle, interwoven, entwined, inextricably bound together. They are real and mythic, primal and archetypal. It is the conflict between good and evil.

Two Brothers Fighting is an old story made new by the artist. It is a tale from the past, told in the present, with intimations of the future. It is a story told by Eduardo Carrillo in his own language, the language of art.

Bernard M. Goldberg
Professor of English and Judaic Studies
and Founder of The Dov-Ber Project

Couple in the Garden
1985
Oil on canvas
48 x 34.25"
Courtesy of the Monterey Museum of Art
Monterey, California

Dwarfed by blue-shadowed hills still unsunned but edged with the luminous promise of early morning light, a couple enters the garden. He leans forward, curious, awed. She pauses reflectively within the sparse outline of a house. Around them, leaves catch the first glint of sunrise, grasses glow at their feet and the upcurved branches of a giant, loose-limbed tree burn with an ethereal light. *Couple in the Garden* holds within it the essence of Eduardo

Carrillo's gleaming palette, his fluid, unconventional compositional style, his reverence for nature and his ability to invoke archetype and myth. It also contains a key to his genius for relationships.

Earthy but filled with light, the man and woman are each their own; they do not dominate but approach with wonder and respect; in this painting they are in harmonious rhythm with each other and with the exuberance of nature that surrounds them. In the presence of such abundance and magic, they are not afraid: this is how the artist moved through his own life—unafraid, reverent, awe-full, mirthful.

Within his Garden, the gods are vividly present. Over the scene, a totemic Tree of Life or Ojo de Dios-menorah-Holy Ghost expresses a benevolent life force.

Alison has said that Carrillo saw life in layers of reality. Certainly he found deep magic within whatever and whomever he addressed. Anything, anyone was worthy of his attention and, in the light of his attention, became majestic. Indeed, like his figures outlined in pearly luminescence, he illuminated people's gifts. They recognized and claimed these gifts, and loved him for it.

Maureen Davidson
Writer and Independent Curator

You paint
Like a confession

Paleo dreams slight of sight
Artifact as artfact

Exhumed

You use speculations
Arbitrary signs and symbols
Astronomy biology chemistry
Mathematics medicine physics
Meta this and that

You eat mind marrow

Is it you who
Fled topiary gardens and why and gone
Where?

Tangled clues of amputated stairs
Cleft rainbows wonder walls
Sci fi sky awedeath
Stamen bee monkey

Mas

(you and someone else are responsible for green).

Daymare done
Killer paintings circle art

While you rest and lie
Like Mexico with Egypt under rumbled stars.

Joni Gordon
April 1975

La Candelaria
1988
Oil on canvas
30 x 40"
Collection Anne Chowning Sisney

Ruben and Juliette
1987-1992
Oil on canvas
48 x 54"
Collection Juliette Carrillo and Ruben Carrillo

La Ultima Cena
1994
Oil on canvas
27 x 81"
Collection Alison Carrillo

Fifty-Five Gallon Drum
1991
Oil on canvas
60 x 48"
Private collection

DEDICATORIA CHICANA

al dolor la risa de mi gente
rica en su pobreza, tierna como nopal
florenciendo cantos en el deserto:
a su promesa y olvido me acojo

gente mitotera en los ventanales,
olor de campo, ninos en las puertas,
mujeres a solas desangrandose:
mi voz como balcon de barrio alega

hay tantas prisones, tantos silencios,
tantas muertes negandome la vida:
mis raices tambien de almohada mi sirven

a los que-como yo-nacieron marcados
hechos extranjerosa en su propia tierra:
como patria nueva, mis versos libres

Francisco X. Alarcon
Poet, Professor and Chicano
Literary Prize Awardee

to the grief and laughter of my people,
rich in their poverty, tender as prickly pear
flowering songs in the desert:
I shelter in their promise and neglect

gossipy people in windows of houses,
odor of fields, children in doorways,
women bleeding all alone:
my voice argues like a balcony in the barrio

there are so many prisons, so many silences,
so many deaths forbidding my life,
my roots serve me also as a pillow

to those who-like me-were born branded,
made strangers in their own soil:
here is a new country, my free verses

Translation by **Adrienne Rich**, *with the poet.*
Poet, Professor and MacArthur Fellow

Calle De Locos
1984
Oil on canvas
30 x 33.5"
Collection Alison Carrillo

Altar and Visitor
Oil on canvas
1984
38.5 x 40.5"
Collection Juliette Carrillo

Adagio Doloroso
1992
Oil on Canvas
60 x 48"
Collection Alison Carrillo

Doyle
1992
Oil on canvas
15 x 18"
Collection Doyle and Selma Foreman

Ali's Desert Dream
1991
Oil on canvas
8 x 14"
Collection Alison Carrillo

Tio Beto on the Wall
1987-1988
Oil on canvas
33 × 37"
Collection Alison Carrillo

YOU ARE HERE

Oozing paint
Seeping out cracks
Between life and death

Ooze creeps   puddles
Outing itself visibly

We watch and see

Patiently steadfast

Your art rises again
Molten timid persistent
Resurrection testing history
Laying bare bones of truth

Being Chicano as you are
Had its own Jackel and Hide

You as Hybrid
Life water   trees   cabins   gates
Eruptions   floradora
Lush jumbled jungles
Painted in colors
Swollen gorgeous with beauty

No mas

Living interfered with life
The be stung

Now you begin again
As Eduardo the first
Early on Chicano
The art man bearing paintings
Before history tarted up the wrong art boy

Your art existed in myriad pyramids
Being excavated

Genetics of painting sowed

Beyond doubts   misgivings   betrayals
Actual life stuff
Art endures circumstance
Fixed in times psyche
Where all is remembered

Joni Gordon
May 6, 2009

Ruben
1992
Oil on canvas
50 x 37"
Collection Ruben Carrillo

Leda and the Swan
1996
Oil on canvas
56.5 x 51.5"
Collection Alison Carrillo

Vegetable Man
1997
Oil on canvas
60 x 48"
Collection John and Jane Fitz Gibbon

42

FOR EDUARDO

You broke beauty from the living,
plucked it out of the world like a thorn.
Then pierced your own flesh, blood running
crimson, alizarin, down your palm
painting this kingdom
of Tecate bottles, sliced melon, mongrel dogs,
white stallions rearing, shark fisherman
in pressed guayaberas, their muscled arms at rest,
lovers crumpled on a blanket beside fields of ripening grapes,
the curve of a woman's bare flanks, those purpled boughs of Paradise.

Brush in hand, you stood on a bruised ledge
watching the smoke of breakfast fires rise
over the cradle of San Ignacio. You stumbled
under the stars, strumming your mandolin and singing
to lure mermaids from the sea.
And out they came, glittering with starfish,
dragging seaweed in their tangled hair.

At last, you sit here, hombre vegetal,
sipping your margarita and gazing at the moon
your arm a branch, your lettuce legs,
Brussels sprouts for calves, this life voracious,
devouring, its many hungers, some satisfied
only by a certain shade of green, a thin stroke
of umber, the luminous ache of color
as it lifts off the canvas. You leave us
this certainty, a world alive in your absence,
still dancing, like calaveras on their brightly painted graves,
shaking maracas in their skeletal fists,
marigolds flaming from their mouths.

Danusha Laméris
Poet and Painter

Self Portrait with carved frame
1993
Oil on canvas
33.25 x 27.25" (Carved frame by Clemente Arce Villavicencio)
Collection Alison Carrillo

44

DONORS TO THE CATALOGUE

Alison Carrillo

Wendy Miller

Janet and Walter Miller Fund for Philanthropic Giving

The Museum of Art & History @ the McPherson Center, Santa Cruz, California

Weigand Gallery, College of Notre Dame de Namur, Belmont, California

Santa Rosa Junior College Art Gallery, Santa Rosa, California

LENDERS TO THE EXHIBITION

Alison Carrillo

Juliette Carrillo

Ruben Carrillo

Sheila Carrillo

John and Jane Fitz Gibbon

Doyle and Selma Foreman

Tim Price

Anne Chowning Sisney

Donna and Lee Sweatfield

The Monterey Museum of Art

Private Collections

EDUARDO CARRILLO

BORN

1937, Santa Monica, California

AT REST

1997, San Ignacio, Baja, California

EDUCATION

| 1964 | University of California, Los Angeles Master of Arts |
| 1962 | University of California, Los Angeles Bachelor of Arts |

TEACHING EXPERIENCE

1972-1997	Professor of Art, University of California, Santa Cruz, CA
1971	Assistant Professor of Art, Sacramento State University, CA
1966	Founder and Director, El Centro de Arte Regional La Paz, Baja, CA

MURALIST

1978	Plazita De Dolores, 44 x 8' tile mural, Los Angeles, CA
1976	Palomar Arcade Mural, politec on masonry. Planning and execution of interior architectural painting measuring over 2500 sq. ft., Santa Cruz, CA (Destroyed)
1970	Collaborative Mural in Chicano Library, Campbell Hall, University of California, Los Angeles, CA

CURATOR

| 1982-83 | *Third World Exhibit, ASCO Exhibit*, Sesnon Gallery, University of California, Santa Cruz, CA |
| 1979-1981 | *Califas,* Sesnon Gallery, University of California, Santa Cruz, CA |

Posthumous Solo Exhibitions

2014/15	*Eduardo Carrillo*, Crocker Art Museum, Sacramento, CA
2010	*Eduardo Carrillo,* Santa Rosa Junior College Art Gallery, Santa Rosa, CA
	Eduardo Carrillo, Weigand Gallery, College of Notre Dame de Namur, Belmont, CA
2009	*Eduardo Carrillo: Within a Cultural Context*, Museum of Art and History @ the McPherson Center, Santa Cruz, CA
2008	*La Tierra de Mi Madre, The Land of My Mother*, National Steinbeck Center, Salinas, CA

Posthumous Selected Group Exhibitions

2012	*Los Angeles: The Mexican American Generation: 1945–1965*, Claremont College, Claremont, CA
2007	*Intimate Landscape,* curated by Frank Galuszka, Mary Porter Sesnon Gallery, UCSC
	Christopher Winfield Gallery, Carmel, CA
	California in Connecticut, Joanne and William Rees Collection, New Britain Museum of American Art, New Britain, CT
2002/03	*The Pilot Hill Collection of Contemporary Art,* Crocker Art Museum, Sacramento, CA
2001, 1999, 1997	Joseph Chowning Gallery, San Francisco, CA

Selected Solo Exhibitions

1995	Joseph Chowning Gallery, San Francisco, CA (Numerous solo exhibitions throughout the 80s and 90s)
1988	L.A. Louver Gallery, Venice, CA
1986	Crocker Art Museum, Sacramento, CA
1975	Open Ring Gallery, Sacramento, CA
	California State University, Los Angeles, CA
1972	Brand Art Library, Glendale, CA
	Crocker Art Gallery, Sacramento, CA
1968	Sala de Bellas Artes, La Paz, B.C., Mexico
1965	La Jolla Museum of Contemporary Art, La Jolla, CA
1963	Ceeje Gallery, Los Angeles, CA

SELECTED GROUP EXHIBITIONS

1993   *CARA–Chicano Resistance and Affirmation*, San Antonio Museum of Art, San Antonio, Texas

         Bronx Museum, New York

1992   *Puertas de Luz*, Galeria Nueva, Los Angeles, CA

       CARA–Chicano Resistance and Affirmation, Tucson Museum of Art, Tucson, AZ

         National Museum of American Art, Washington, D.C.

1987   *New Works*, Joseph Chowning Gallery, San Francisco, CA

       The Artist and The Myth, Monterey Peninsula Museum of Art, Monterey, CA

1986   *American European Painting and Sculpture*, L.A. Louver Gallery, Venice, CA

       Heartbeat of a Culture, Mexican Museum of CA

       Six Painters, Triton Museum of Art, Santa Clara, CA

1985   *American/European*, L.A. Louver Gallery, Venice, CA

1984   *Ceeje Gallery Revisited*, Los Angeles Municipal Art Gallery, Los Angeles, CA

1981   *Califas, Chicano Art and Culture in California*, Sesnon Gallery, University of California, Santa Cruz, CA

1980   *Ancient Roots/New Visions*, Palacia de Mineria, Mexico D.F.

       Fuegos de Atzlan, Oakes College, University of California, Santa Cruz, CA

1979   *Ancient Roots/New Vision*, Everson Museum of Art, New York

         Museum of Contemporary Art, Chicago, IL

         San Antonio Museum, TX

1978   *Ancient Roots/New Vision,* Colorado Springs Fine Art Center, CO

         Los Angeles Municipal Art Gallery

         University of Houston, Southwest Chicano Arts Center, TX

       Bad Painting, New Museum, New School of Social Research, New York, NY

       Early Sixties at UCLA, Fredrick S. Wight Art Gallery, University of California, Los Angeles, CA

1968   Invitational, Mexico Instituto National de Bellas Artes

1967   *Four Painters,* California State University, Hayward, CA

1966   *California '66,* Crocker Art Gallery, Sacramento, CA

       Inaugural Exhibition, Fine Arts Facilities, Palomar College, San Marcos, CA

       Painting–The Introspective Image, Long Beach Museum, Long Beach, CA (multiple national venues)

       Polychrome Sculpture, Long Beach Museum of Art, Long Beach, CA

1964   *Six Painters of the Rear Guard,* Ceeje Gallery, Los Angeles, CA

     Annual Exhibition, Whittier College, Whittier, CA

     Three Man Show, Rolf Nelson Gallery, Los Angeles, CA

SELECTED PUBLICATIONS

2006   *Art of Engagement–Visual Politics in California and Beyond,* Peter Selz

      San Jose Museum of Art, CA

2002/03 *The Pilot Hill Collection of Contemporary Art,* Crocker Art Museum, Sacramento, CA

1995   *Temporarily Possessed: The Semi-Permanent Collection,* Brian Goldfarb, John Hatfield,

      Laura Trippi and Mimi Young, The New Museum of Contemporary Art, New York, NY

1991   *CARA: Chicano Art: Resistance and Affirmation 1965-1985,* Richard Griswold del Castillo, University of

      Arizona Press, AZ

1990   *California A-Z and Return,* John Fitz Gibbon, Butler Institute of American Art, Youngstown, OH

1989   *The Circuit,* Francisco Jimenez, McDougal Littell Reading Literature, Geneva, IL

     Mano a Mano, Rolando Castellon, Oakland Museum of Art, Oakland, CA

1988   *Murals of Los Angeles: The Big Picture,* photographs by Melba Lavick, commentary by Stanley Young,

      Published by Little Brown and Co. New York, NY

     The Latin American Spirit: Art and Artists in the United States 1920-1970, Luis R. Cancel, Bronx Museum

      of Art, Harry Abrams, New York, NY

1986   *Art in the San Francisco Bay Area 1945-1980,* Thomas Albright, University of California Press, Berkeley, CA

     Arte Chicano, Thomas Ybarra Frausto, Shifra Goldstein, University of California Press, CA

     Eduardo Carrillo, Crocker Art Museum, Sacramento, CA

1985   *Made in Atzlan–Chicano Art from the Southwest,* Phillip Brookman, Tomas Ybarra Frausto, Centro

      Cultural De La Raza, San Diego, CA

1984   *Ceeje Revisited,* Los Angeles Municipal Art Gallery, Josine Ianco Starrels, Susan B. Larsen, Fidel Danieli,

      Faith Flam, Los Angeles, CA

1978   *Bad Painting,* New Museum, Marcia Tucker, New York, NY

     The Early Sixties at UCLA, Fredrick Wight Gallery, University of California, Los Angeles, CA

1975   *Selected Works From 1960-1975,* Aron Goldberg, Joni Gordon, Los Angeles Fine Arts Gallery, California

      State University, Los Angeles, CA

SELECTED PUBLIC AND PRIVATE COLLECTIONS

Dr. Leon Banks and Family

Tony Berlant

William and Teresa Bourke

Alison Carrillo

Juliette Carrillo

Ruben Carrillo

Sheila Carrillo

The Carrillo Family

Joseph Chowning

John and Jane Fitz Gibbon

Joni and Monte Gordon

Roger Hollander

Tim Price

William and Joanne Rees

Anne Chowning Sisney

Donna and Lee Sweatfield

The Capitol Group, Los Angeles, CA

Crocker Art Museum, Sacramento, CA

Corpus Christi Museum, Corpus Christi, Texas

De Langes, Mitchell and Linden, San Francisco, CA

Oakland Museum of Art, Oakland, CA

Monterey Museum of Art, Monterey, CA

Mexican Museum, San Francisco, CA

The New Museum of Contemporary Art, New York, NY

Yale University, New Haven, CT

Private Collections

CONTRIBUTORS

Francisco X. Alarcon is a Chicano poet and educator who teaches at University of California, Davis. He has published numerous volumes of poetry. In 1993 his bi-lingual poems for children were transformed into songs by his colleague Pablo Ortiz under the auspices of grants from MEXUS and the Rockefeller Foundation. The winner of numerous awards, including The Chicano Literary Prize and the Fred Cody Lifetime Achievement Award.

Betsy Andersen is Director of Museo Eduardo Carrillo. She is a painter. As co-director of Woven Stories, Woven Lives, she works with diverse age groups and constituencies to create community based public art murals, giving visibility and voice to those groups.

Alison Carrillo founded Museo Eduardo Carrillo in 2001 in order to promote the art and legacy of her husband, Eduardo Carrillo.

Maureen Davidson is an art writer for publications including Artweek, independent curator, co-director of Anton Gallery in Monterey and active cultural worker. She has been Deputy Director of Long Beach Museum of Art, Executive Director of Ventura Arts Council and of Spokane Art School, and served as panelist for state and local grants.

Paul Figueroa is Director of The Museum of Art & History @ the MacPherson Center, Santa Cruz, California. His long tenure at The Gibbs Museum of Art in Charleston, South Carolina included serving as Curator of Education (1976-1988) and Executive Director (1988-2002). His own interest in photography brings a personal empathy to the arts.

Bernard M. Goldberg is Professor of English and Associate Professor of Jewish Studies at West Los Angeles College, where he led the Creative Writing in Prague and Creative Writing in Jerusalem Programs. He has had short stories published and plays produced. He wrote and directed the short film "The Last Day" and founded the Dov Ber Project, a non-profit organization created to help produce art that is influenced by Jewish thought and culture.

Joni Gordon is a poet. She has been an arts advocate for more than a quarter of a century through her gallery, Newspace, a Los Angeles landmark. Ms. Gordon continues to champion artists. Her contributions and insights are documented through a series of oral history interviews on the Smithsonian Institute's website, Archives of American Art. She knew Eduardo Carrillo during their time at UCLA in the 1960s.

Susan Hillhouse, Curator of Exhibitions and Collections for The Museum of Art & History @ the McPherson Center in Santa Cruz, California, has been in the art and museum field for over twenty years. In addition to her museum work, Hillhouse teaches Western and Eastern art history survey classes at West Valley College in Saratoga, California.

Danusha Laméris's poems have appeared in a number of journals and anthologies, including *Crab Orchard Review, El Andar, Alaska Quarterly Review* and *Poetry Northwest*. She lives in Santa Cruz, California and, for two years, studied painting with Eduardo Carrillo at UCSC.

Dr. Amalia Mesa-Bains is an artist whose work is deeply rooted in Chicano culture. She is credited with re-interpreting the traditional shrine into a contemporary idiom. A scholar and nationally known lecturer on Latino Art, she is the recipient of the MacArthur Fellowship. Currently she is Director of the Department of Visual and Public Art at California State University, Monterey Bay.

Adrienne Rich is a poet, essayist and feminist. She is considered one of the most influential writers of our time because her transformational poetry speaks to the conflictual themes in our lives. including sexuality, aging and social conscience. Her commitment to broad social issues has earned her numerous awards, including the MacArthur Fellowship and the National Poetry Association Award for Distinguished Service to the Art of Poetry.

Robert Poplack is Professor of Art, and is the Director and Curator of the Wiegand Gallery at Notre Dame de Namur University in Belmont, CA. He is a practicing painter who has had numerous solo shows and has also been included in many group exhibitions nationally.

Roberta Ruiz is a painter and teacher of art. A graduate of Stanford University and recipient of California Arts Council grants, she has taught extensively within alternative environments like Soledad Prison, Larkin Street Youth Center and The National Steinbeck Center, as well as University of California, Santa Cruz.

Stephanie Sanchez is a painter and educator. She was located in Southern California for some time, teaching at numerous art institutions there. Currently living and working in Petaluma, she teaches painting and drawing at Santa Rosa Junior College Art department. Her most recent show of California Landscape was at Terence Rogers Fine Art in Santa Monica, California

Christina Waters uses her PhD in Philosophy to lecture in the Arts and Humanities at UC Santa Cruz. She is a longtime Bay Area journalist specializing in writing about food, wine and the arts, and is the author of a travel guide to the Central Coast of California. A passionate plein aire painter and 6th generation Californian, she lives in Santa Cruz.